The Concise Political Dictionary

BookCap™ Study Guides

www.bookcaps.com

Table of Contents

A

abdication [ab-di-key-shun] -noun- The act of renouncing

abrogation [ab-ruh-gey-shun] -noun- The act of repealing or an insistence to do so

absolutism [ab-suh-loo-tiz-uhm] -noun- The principle of maintaining complete and unrestricted power within the government

academic freedom [ak-uh-dem-ik free-dum] -noun- A teacher's or student's freedom to inquire without fear of punishment

accord [uh-kord] -verb- To be in total agreement or harmony

acculturation [uh-kul-chuh-rey-shun] -noun- The process of one group of people adopting the social behaviors and practices of another group of people

Achilles' [uh-kil-eez] -noun- The greatest Greek warrior in the Trojan War

---
4

acid test [ass-id test] -noun- Parties held by Ken Kessey and the Merry Pranksters advocating the use of LSD

adjournment [uh-jurn-muhnt] -noun- The closing of court after the end of a session

adjudication [uh-joo-duh-kay-shun] -noun- In court, the act of making a judgment or a decree

administration [ad-min-uh-stray-shun] -noun- The act of a government exercising its political duties

adversary system [ad-ver-sar-ee sis-tems]] -noun- The trial practice in which both sides are given opportunity to present their case, as practiced in the United States

aegis [ee-jis] -noun- Doing something under the watch of a powerful and knowledgeable source

affidavit [af-i-day-vit] -noun- A declaration which is written under oath and in the presence of an official

affirmative action [af-fer-muh-tiv ak-shun] -noun- An act to ensure that women and minority members are treated equally, especially in a work environment

affluent [af-loo-uhnt] -adj- A person with an extreme amount of wealth, material possessions, and resources

aggregate demand [ag-re-get dee-mand] -noun- Given the time and price level, the total amount of demand for a product within an economy

aggregate supply [ag-re-get sup-lie] -noun- Given the time and price level, the total amount of goods which are produced within an economy

agitprop [aj-it-prop] -noun- An office which negotiates agitation and propaganda, which may especially be related to Communism

agrarian [ug-grair-ee-uhn] -adj- As related to the division of land or land tenure

ahistorical [ay-his-tor-i-kal] -adj- Indifferent to historical significance or development

aide de camp [ayd-duh-kamp] -noun- A subordinate military officer who acts as a confidential advocate to a higher official

allegiance [uh-lee-juhns] -noun- The loyalty of a person to their government or sovereign alliance [uh-lie-uhns] -noun- Individuals, families, or organizations merging their efforts to act as one

altruism [al-troo-iz-uhm] -noun- A person who practices unselfish concern for other groups of people or organizations

ambassador [am-bas-uh-der] -noun- A high-ranking diplomatic official who acts as a representative for the entire country in foreign matters

amnesty [am-nuh-stee] -noun- A general pardon for offenses, especially those against the government

anarchy   [an-er-kee] -noun- A society which is void of any law or government

annexation [an-ik-say-shun] -noun- The act of a state proclaiming sovereignty over a land outside of its territory

anthropology [an-thro-pol-uh-jee] -noun- The study of the differences and similarities between humans and animals

Anti-ballistic Missle Treaty (ABM) [ann-tie bal-iz-tik miss-el tree-tee] -noun- A treaty between the United States and the Soviet Union which regulates the use of the anti-ballistic missile systems in defense against nuclear warfare

anti-clericalism [an-tee-klair-ik-al-iz-m] -noun- A person's opposition to the teachings and practices of the church

anti-communism [an-tee-kom-yoo-niz-m] -noun- A person's opposition to an environment which is controlled in a totalitarian manner

anti-Semitism [an-tee-sem-it-iz-m] -noun- Discrimination, prejudice, or hostility toward the Jewish people

anti-trust laws [an-tee-trust law-z] -noun- Laws which are aimed at forces businesses and business owners to compete fairly with one another

apolitical [ey-puh-li-tik-uhl] -adj- Anything that is not political or is opposed to politics

apologist [uh-pol-uh-jist] -noun- A person who defends their beliefs and ideas in writing

—

appeasement [uh-peez-ment] -noun- The act of pacifism, such as creating an environment which is peaceful

appropriation [uh-pro-pree-ey-shun] -noun- The authorization of using money from the treasury for a specified use, by legislation

arbitrary [ar-buh-trair-ee] -adj- Subject to the judgment of an individual rather than a jury, such as a judge

aristocracy [ar-uh-stok-ruh-see] -noun- People who are considered to be the most noble in society

armistice [ahr-muh-stis] -noun- Between warring parties, an agreement for temporary suspension of hostile activities

atavism   [at-uh-viz-uhm] -noun- The reappearance of certain traits which have been absent for some time

austerity [aw-stair-i-tee] -noun- The severity of certain manners

autarchy [aw-tahr-kee] -noun- A government with absolute sovereignty

authoritarian [aw-thaur-i-ter-ee-uhn] -adj- An
absolute obedience to a leader, which discourages
individual freedom

autocracy [aw-tok-ruh-see] -noun- A governmental
structure in which one individual has absolute power

automation [aw-tuh-may-shun] -noun- The electronic
control of equipment or a system

autonomy [aw-ton-uh-mee] -noun- A society which is
self-governed by independent and free people

B

balance of payments [bal-uhns uhv pae-mentz] -noun-
The difference between payments to and receipts
from foreign countries

balance of terror [bal-uhns uhv tair-or] -noun- The
fair distribution of nuclear weapons between
countries so that no country will attack another for
fear that they will be retaliated against

balance of trade [bal-uhns uhv trayd] -noun- A
difference between the values of imports and exports
in a country

balkanization [bawl-kuh-nie-zay-shun] -noun- The division of a country into small states which conflict with one another

belligerency [buh-lij-er-uhn-see] -noun- The position of being actively participating and engaged in war

bicameral [bi-kam-er-uhl] -adj- A legislative body with two houses or divisions

bicameral government [bi-kam-er-uhl guv-ern-ment] -noun- A government in which two camels, or divisions, make the legislative decisions

big stick [big stik] -noun- A policy created by President Theodore Roosevelt in response to the Monroe Doctrine; to negotiate peacefully while simultaneously threatening with the "big stick" of a military

bilateral [bi-lat-er-uhl] -adj- Something, as an agreement, which pertains to and affects both parties involved

bipartisan [bi-par-tuh-suhn] -adj- Inclusive of members from both parties involved black consciousness [blak con-shus-ness] -noun- An awareness of and pride in one's identity as a black person

blacklist [blak-list] -noun- A list of people who are under suspicion

bloc [blok] -noun- A group of legislators representing multiple political parties who meet together to discuss an issue

block voting [blok vo-ting] -noun- A voting system which results in multiple winners and has a checkbox ballot

Bolshevism [bohl-shuh-viz-uhm] -noun- The principles practiced by social figures or politicians who are ultra radical

bourgeois [boor-zwa-zee] -noun- A person who allows their social, economic, and political opinions to be dictated by material values and social standings

breach of the peace [breech uhv tha peese] -noun- A riot, public disturbance, or any other act which threatens public peace

brigandage [brig-uhn-daj] -noun- The act of stealing or mugging, as a bandit

brinkmanship [bringk-muhn-ship] -noun- The political technique of giving the impression that one is willing to push an issue which may be highly dangerous to the absolute limit, rather than backing down

Bush Doctrine [boo'sh dok-trin] -noun- A phrase used to describe the various foreign policy principles of President George W. Bush, though initially it described the policy that the US had the right to secure itself against countries that harbor or give aid to terrorist groups

business cycle [biz-ness si-kul] -noun- A country's fluctuating business economy, recurrently

by-election [bi-il-ek-shun] -noun- When there is a vacancy in Parliament, a special election held at a time other than normally scheduled elections

C

cadre   [kad-ree] -noun- A group of qualified personnel who are capable of leading an organization which is in expanded form caliphate [kal-uh-fayt] -noun- The jurisdiction of a spiritual leader of Islam

canon law [kay-nan law] -noun- The body of laws and regulations which are used in the governing of Christian organizations

Capitalism [kap-uh-tal-iz-m] -noun- An economic system in which any production or distribution is owned and dictated by corporate forces

capitulation [kuh-pich-uh-lay-shun] -noun- To surrender or to give up, or a document which states the terms of surrender

carpetbagger [kar-pet-bag-er] -noun- Any outsider who is considered to be opportunistic or exploitative

carte blanche [kahrt blanch] -noun- To have total and unconditional authority

Carter Doctrine[kar-ter dok-trin] -noun- A policy introduced by President Jimmy Carter stating that the United States would employ military force if needed in the protection of the Persian Gulf, in order to protect its interests in that area

---

caste [kast] -noun- Any social class which shares cultural aspects and beliefs

casus belli [kass-us bell-ee] -noun- A justification for the acts of war

centralization [sen-truh-lie-zay-shun] -noun- The concentration of authority or administrative control within a central government

centrism [sen-triz-m] -noun- The act of taking a moderate political position, rather than being extreme left or right

charter [char-ter] -noun- A document which dictates the principles and functions of any corporate body; a constitution

chauvinism [sho-vuh-niz-m] -noun- A devotion to any group or cause which is biased

Christian Democrats [kris-chuhn dem-uh-krats] -noun- A group of people who wish to apply the principles of Christianity to public policy

civil disobedience [si-vil dis-oh-bee-dee-ents] -noun- An active refusal to obey laws or government commands

civil liberties [si-vil li-ber-tees] -noun- Individual rights and freedoms which pertain to certain groups, such as slaves or women

civil war [si-vil war] -noun- A war within a country

civitas [siv-i-tas] -noun- The citizens who impart a shared responsibility within a commonwealth or city-state, especially

clan [klan] -noun- A group of people who are descended from a common source, or a social clique with a common goal

class [klass] -noun- A group which forms due to common characteristics or traits

class struggle [klass struh-gul] -noun- Class conflict observed from the socialist perspective

classical economics [klass-uh-kuhl ek-uh-nom-iks] -noun- Active until the mid-19th century, the first school of modern economic thinking

clemency [klem-uhn-see] -noun- The act of being merciful or lenient closed shop [klohzd shop] -noun- An agreement by employers to hire only union members

closure [kloh-zhur] -noun- Reaching a conclusion

coalition [koh-uh-lish-uhn] -noun- A combined alliance between persons or states which is likely only temporary

code [kohd] -noun- A collection of laws or standards which are systematically arranged

codification [kohd-uh-fuh-kay-shun] -noun- The process involved when forming or writing legal code

coercion [koh-er-shun] -noun- The act of the government or police using forceful means to achieve compliance

coexistence [ko-ig-zis-tuhns] -noun- Nations, people, or cultures living peacefully with one another despite any agreements that may arise

cohort [ko-hawrt] -noun- An accomplice, associate, or companion

collaboration [kuh-lab-uh-ray-shun] -noun- The act of two or more people working together on one unified effort

collective bargaining [kuh-lek-tiv bar-gun-ing] -noun- The process of employers and groups of employees negotiating working conditions

collective responsibility [kuh-lek-tiv ree-spon-si-bil-uh-tee] -noun- Every member of a group takes responsibility and accepts punishment for the actions and decision making of individual members

collective security [kuh-lek-tiv si-kyoor-uh-tee] -noun- An arrangement in which each member of a system accepts and agrees that the security of each member is the concern of the group as a whole

collectivism [kuh-lek-tiv-iz-m] -noun- A political, economic, or social agreement that decisions will be made by the group as a collective rather than by individuals and all decisions will be made with the group as a whole in mind

collegialism [kuh-lee-jul-iz-m] -noun- The idea that the church is separate from and equal to the state

Cominform [kom-in-fohrm] -noun- Nine European parties which came together under Communism to form a coordinated advisory

Comintern [kom-in-tern] -noun- Also known as Third International, a united front of Communist parties who would like to push forth the principles of Communism by means of a violent revolution

commissar [kom-uh-sahr] -noun- A high official of the Communist party who is in charge of enforcing the bounds of party loyalty

Communist Manifesto [kom-yoo-nest man-uh-fes-sto] -noun- A publication written by Karl Marx and Friedrich Engels which lays out the program and purposes of the Communist League

conciliation [kon-sil-ee-ay-shun]-verb-To appease, or to try to regain friendship or trust by means of pleasant behaviors

conscientious objector [kon-she-en-shus ob-jek-tor] -noun- A person's refusal to participate in the military or to bear arms based on religious or moral obligations conscription [kon-skrip-shun] -noun- A compulsory action in the time of war, such as a draft or a contribution of money

consensus agreement [kon-sen-sis uh-gree-ment] -noun- A judgment or opinion which is reached by an entire group, rather than an individual

consortium [kon-sor-shee-uhm] -noun- A partnership or union, especially in terms of financial institutions and capitalism

conspicuous consumption [kon-spik-yoo-us kon-sump-shun] -noun- The excessive spending of an individual or company for the sole purpose of making their wealth known

constitutional monarchy [kon-stuh-too-shun-uhl mon-ark-ee] -noun- A government which is headed by a monarch who has to work within the parameters of a constitution

contempt of court [kon-tempt uhv kort] -noun- An order which declares that an individual has been disloyal or disrespectful of the court's authority

counter culture   [kown-ter kul-chur] -noun- The values of a certain culture or group which counter the mainstream values of that time

___

counter revolution [kown-ter rev-uh-loo-shun] -noun- A revolution against the government when that government recently came into effect by a revolution

coup d'etat [koo day-tah] -noun- In politics, a sudden action which results in the government changing, possibly illegally or forcefully

D

dark horse [dahrk hoors] -noun- In politics, a candidate who no one expects to win but does

de facto [dee fak-toh] -noun- A fact or a reality; something which actually exists

de jure [dee joor-ee] -noun- Something which exists by right or according to a lie

demagogue [dem-uh-gog] -noun- A leader of the people, in politics, who can gain support and power of the people by arousing their emotions and prejudices

democracy [duh-mok-ruh-see] -noun- A government which is comprised of political and social equality and in which leaders are chosen by the people

demographics [dem-uh-graf-iks] -noun- The statistics of a population, such as ages, education levels, and income levels

despot [des-pot] -noun- A ruler who has unlimited and oppressive power, as a king or tyrant

devolution [dev-uh-loo-shun] -noun- The passing or inheritance of a property from one owner to another in succession

direct action [di-rekt ak-shun] -noun- An action which is made with the intention of getting a direct and immediate result

direct democracy [di-rekt duh-mok-ruh-see] -noun- A form of government in which the people vote directly on policies, as opposed to a regular democracy when the people will vote on representatives who will vote on policie

dissident [dis-i-duhnt] -noun- A person who disagrees

dogma [dog-muh] -noun- A principle or belief especially as related to morality or faith domino theory [dom-uh-no theer-ee] -noun- The idea that if one state adopted a Communist government then other states would follow one by one

double jeopardy [duh-bul jep-ar-dee] -noun- The rule that a person, once convicted or acquitted, cannot be tried again on the same charges

draconian laws   [druh-koh-nee-an lawz] -noun- A set of laws which are said to be exceedingly severe, or to be "written in blood"

drawback [draw-bak] -noun- A refund tariff which comes about when imported good are reexported

due process [doo prah-ses] -noun- The way the law is administered, such that no citizen's right will be violated, legal principles will be followed, and the accused has every right to face his/her accuser

dumping [duhmp-ing]-verb-The act of dismissing, firing, or releasing a person from a contract

dyed in the wool [dayhd in thuh woo'l] -noun- Something which is complete or through-and-through

E

ecclesiastical [ih-klee-zee-az-tik-uhl] -adj- A thing which pertains to the church or clergy

ecology   [ih-kol-uh-jee] -noun- The biological study of the way organisms interact with their environment

ecumenical [ek-yoo-men-i-kuhl] -adj- Something which is known to the general public, or universal

ecumenism [ek-yoo-muh-niz-uhm] -noun- Initiatives which were aimed at forming a united Christian front

greenhouse effect [green-howse uh-fekt] -noun- A process by which radiation is absorbed by greenhouse gases and re-radiated back into the lower atmosphere where it causes temperature increases

egalitarianism [ih-gal-uh-tair-ee-an-iz-uhm] -noun- A belief that all people are equal, especially in terms of socialism, politics, or economics

eleventh hour [ee-lev-inth ow-er] -noun- The absolute last possible moment that it is possible to do something

elite [ih-leet] -adj- A person or group of people who share power of the highest authority

emeritus [ih-mer-i-tuhs] -adj- A person who still holds their title even after being dismissed from a position

emigration [em-uh-gray-shun] -noun- The act of leaving a country for the purpose of settling in another country

eminent domain [em-uh-nent do-mayn] -noun- The state's power to take over private property to use for a public purpose if they compensate the owner

enclave   [en-clayv] -noun- A small group or area which is enclosed inside of another larger area, where it is isolated

entente [ahn-tahnt] -noun- When two or more nations make an agreement to abide by certain policies when it comes to international affairs

envoy [ahn-voi] -noun- An agent of diplomacy

ethnocentrism [eth-no-sen-triz-uhm] -noun- The belief that one's culture or beliefs are superior to another's

ethos [ee-ts] -noun- The fundamentals of a certain
culture, such as its characteristics, customs, or beliefs

extradition [ek-struh-dish-uhn] -noun- The surrender
of a fugitive or criminal from one jurisdiction to
another

exile [eg-sahyloun-When a person is banished from
their homeland

expansionism [ek-span-shun-iz-uhm] -noun- The
policy of a nation pertaining to economical or
territorial expansion

Eurocommunism [yu-ro-kom-yoo-niz-uhm] -noun- A
branch of Communism which developed outside of
the Soviet Union, in western Europe

ex-officio [eks-uh-fish-ee-oh] -noun- By virtue of
official position

exploitation [ek-sploi-tay-shun] -noun- The utilization
of a person or thing for the purpose of making a profit

expropriation [eks-pro-pree-ay-shun] -noun- To take
something from another person for one's own
personal use

F

Fabianism [fey-bee-un-iz-uhm] -noun- The Fabian
Society's theories of social and economic reform

faction [fak-shun] -noun- A clique within a larger
clique, such as a governmental party or organization

fait accompl [fe ta-kawn-plee]   noun-In French,
something which has already been accomplished

fascism   [fash-iz-uhm] -noun- A governmental
system which is led by a person who has complete
power

featherbedding [feth-er-bed-ing] -noun- When an
employer is required to hire workers that they do not
need to fill jobs that are unnecessary because of union
terms

federalism [fed-er-uh-liz-uhm] -noun- The principle
of government which unites the states under a central
government rather than individual governments

feudalism [fyood-l-iz-uhm] -noun- The principles of
the feudal system, which existed during the Middle
Ages

fiat [fee-aht] -noun- An order or decree given by a person who has the authority to make sure it is enforced, as a king

fifth column [fith kol-um] -noun- People who act as traitors toward their country because they feel sympathetic for the enemy

fourth estate [forth eh-stayt] -noun- A group of people who wields influence in politics, outside of the usual political powers

front organizations [fruhnt or-gun-i-zay-shuns] -noun- An organization which is set up and controlled by another organization

fundamentalism [fun-duh-men-tl-iz-uhm] -noun- The idea that the bible serves as a literal historical account; a movement in Protestantism in the early 1900s

G

gag rule [gag rool] -noun- A rule which restricts people from debating or discussing openly on some given issue

general strike [jen-er-uhl stryk] -noun- A mass strike in many different industries throughout many different areas of the country

gerontocracy [jer-uhn-tok-ruh-see] -noun- A government which is overseen or ruled by a group of elders

gerrymander [jer-i-man-der] -noun- The division or a state or county into election districts

Gordian knot [gawr-dee-uhn not] -noun- A knot which was tied by Gordius and was said to only be undone by the person who would become the ruler of Asia, but ended up being cut by Alexander the Great

graft [graft] -noun- In surgery, a portion of skin or living tissue which is transplanted from one person to another or from one section of a person's body to another

grandstanding [grand-stand-ing]-verb-A person who acts ostentatiously with the purpose of showing off to others

guild [gild] -noun- A group of people who have related interests and who work together, especially for protection or aid

H

habeas corpus [hey-bee-uhs kawr-puhs] -noun- An order for a person to be brought in front of a judge to determine lawful imprisonment

hack [hak] -verb-To injure or damage a person or thing by use of cruel or insensitive treatment

hegemony [hej-uh-moh-nee] -noun- When one nation has significant influence over other nations

hierarchy [hy-uh-rahr-kee] -noun- A system in which people or things are ranked one over another

holocaust [hol-uh-kawst] -noun- A great sacrifice or complete devastation which is likely caused by fire

I

iconoclastic [ahy-kon-uh-klas-tik] -adj- The breaking or destruction of certain iconic images, especially those which are religious in nature

idealism [ahy-dee-uh-liz-uhm] -noun- The act of cherishing or pursuing more noble purposes and goals ideology [ahy-dee-ol-uh-jee] -noun- A doctrine or belief which an individual, group, or social movement

imperialism [im-peer-ee-uh-liz-uhm] -noun- The process of extending the rule of a country over other foreign countries

in vogue [in vohg] -adj- Something which is within the current trend

incrementalism [in-kruh-men-tl-iz-uhm] -noun- The process of making changes, such as social changes, gradually in increments rather than all at once

independent counsel [in-dee-pen-dent kown-sil] -noun- An official who is appointed at the request of the Attorney General to investigate claims that crimes have been committed by other government officials

indexation [in-dek-say-shun] -noun- Wages, taxes, interest rates, etc. are automatically adjusted to compensate for inflation or a change in the cost of living

indoctrination [in-dok-truh-nay-shun] -noun- Teaching a doctrine, ideology, or principle especially one which is specific to one area such as a religious doctrine

INF Treaty [tree-tee] -noun- A treaty signed between the United States and the Soviet Union in 1987 which eliminated ballistic and cruise missiles, both nuclear and conventional, with an intermediate range

Infidel [in-fi-del] -noun- A person who does not follow a religious faith, especially one who does not follow Christianity

infiltration [in-fil-tray-shun] -noun- In the military, a method of making an attack which involves small groups of soldiers crossing the enemy line at an unguarded or only lightly guarded point

insurrection [in-suh-rek-shun] -noun- An act of revolting or rebelling against an already established government or civil authority

integration [in-tuh-gray-shun] -noun- The act or insistence of joining in with a group, such as a religion or culture, to make a whole

internationalis [in-ter-nash-uhn-al-iz-uhm] -noun- Cooperation amongst nations for the greater good of all parties involved

interventionism [in-ter-ven-shuh-niz-uhm] -noun- A policy which allows the government to interfere in the affairs of other states or in domestic economic issues

———

isolationism [ahy-suh-lay-shun-iz-uhm] -noun- A country's policy of not intervening in the affairs of other countries by staying away from any foreign commitments such as alliances

ivory tower [ahy-vuh-ree tow-er] -noun- Something which remains distant from or shows a disregard toward foreign affairs

J

Jacobinism [jak-uh-bin-iz-uhm] -noun- A policy of extreme radicalism in politics; supporters promoted the Reign of Terror in the late-1700s

Jeffersonian democracy [jef-er-soh-nee-uhn dem-ok-ruh-see] -noun- A movement led by President Thomas Jefferson which called for increased democracy

jihad [ji-hahd] -noun- In Islam, a holy war which is seen as a sacred duty for Muslim's to undertake

jingoism [jing-goh-iz-uhm] -noun- The practice or policy of people who are excessive in the expression of their patriotism and favor war and aggressive foreign policy junta [hoon-tuh] -noun- A small group of people who becomes the ruling party of a country, especially between a coup d'etat and the appointment of a legally constituted government

jurisprudence [joor-is-prood-ns] -noun- A department of law, a system of laws, or the philosophy of law

K

Keynesianism [keyn-zee-uhn-iz-uhm] -noun- A school of economic thought based on the theories of John Maynard Keynes which advocates a mixed economy

kitchen cabinet [kich-uhn cab-uh-net] -noun- The unofficial advisers that Andrew Jackson consulted after he made the unprecedented dismissal of five of his eight official Cabinet members

L

labor movement [lay-ber moov-ment] -noun- Labor unions as a collective; any organizations or individuals who fight for better labor conditions

laissez faire [les-ey fair] -noun- A theory that the government should interfere as little as possible in the economy

landlocked [land-lokt] -adj- A piece of land which is entirely, or almost entirely, surrounded by other pieces of land and has little or no access to the sea

layman [ley-muhn] -noun- A person who is not a member of any given profession, but especially of the clergy

left wing [left wing] -noun- Members of a radical liberal political group

legitimation [luh-jit-uh-may-shun] -noun- The act of making something lawful or in accordance with the established standards

libertarianism [lib-er-tair-ee-uhn-iz-uhm -noun- A policy of maintaining the concept and practice of free will

limited government [lim-i-tid guv-urn-ment] -noun- A government in which governmental intervention in terms of the economy and personal liberties is almost entirely disallowed

limited war [lim-i-tid war] -noun- A war in which not all resources as used and the aim is to not entirely defeat the opponent

M

Machiavellian [mak-ee-uh-vel-ee-uhn] -adj- A government which is characterized by unscrupulous dishonesty, expediency, or cunning as illustrated in Machiavelli's "The Prince"

macroeconomics [mak-roh-ek-uh-nom-iks] -noun- The branch of economics which deals with the broad spectrum of the national economy and the relationship between investments and income within the country as a whole

Malthusian [mal-thoo-zee-uhn] -adj- Pertaining to the beliefs of T.R. Mathus which state that the population increases faster than supplies and sustenance, therefore if there is not war or famine to keep the population in check there will not be enough supplies to support everyone

Marxism [marks-iz-uhm] -noun- A system of socio-economic thought brought forth by Karl Marx and Friedrich Engels which states that capitalism will eventually be overtaken by socialism and a totally classless society

matriarchy [may-tree-ark-ee] -noun- A family or community which is led by women

McCarthyism [muh-kahr-thee-is-uhm] -noun- Making accusations of Communist activity which is generally not supported by any proof

mercantilism [mer-kuhn-til-iz-uhm] -noun- Commercialism in practice or in spirit

mercenary [mer-suh-ner-ee] -noun- A professional soldier who is hired to serve in the army of a foreign country

meritocracy [mer-uh-tok-ruh-see] -noun- Professionals who progress because of talent rather than because of social standing or wealth

messianism [mess-ee-uhn-iz-uhm] -noun- The belief that a cause, a leader, or an ideology will be a savior, such as the Messiah

microeconomics [mahy-kroh-ek-uh-nom-iks] -noun- A more specific view of the economy based on individual firms, consumers, and households

millenarianism [mil-len-ahyr-ee-uhn-iz-uhm] -noun-
Also called millennialism; the belief by certain
groups of people that society will undergo a major
transformation based on a cycle of one thousand years

mixed economy [mikst ee-kon-uh-mee] -noun- An
economy which embraces the public as well as
private elements of enterprise

modus operandi [moh-duhs op-uh-ran-dee] -noun- A
method or mode of working or operating

modus vivendi [moh-duhs vi-ven-dee] -noun- A way
of living or a lifestyle

monetarism [mon-i-tuh-riz-uhm] -noun- A doctrine
which states that the money supply in a nation
dictates where the economy will head

money supply [muh-nee suh-ply] -noun- The sum of
currency or checking-account deposits which are in
circulation

monism   [mon-iz-uhm] -noun- The
consolidating of all processes and concepts into one
single principle of governing

Monroe Doctrine [mon-row dok-trin] -noun- A policy create by President Monroe which forbids involvement in independent nations of the Western hemisphere and also any further colonization of European nations

muckraking [muk-rey-king] -verb- The process of looking for an exposing any corruption within politics, whether it is real or only alleged

mudslinging [muhd-sling-ing] -noun- A person using scandal or maliciousness to discredit another person or competitor

multilateralism   [muhl-ti-lat-uh-ral-iz-uhm] - noun- The act of something being participated in by more than two nations or parties at once

multinational corporations [muhl-ti-nash-uh-nal kor-por-ay-shun] -noun- A corporation which handles business in more than one nation

multipolar [muhl-ti-poh-ler] -adj- Something having more than two poles, possibly many

Muslim Brotherhood [muz-lum bruh-ther-hood] - noun- An Islamic organization which is one of the largest in Islam and the oldest in the world

N

Napoleonic law [nuh-po-lee-on-ik law] -noun- A code
introduced by Napoleon which insisted jobs be given
out based on qualification, people be free to practice
whatever religion they choose, and no one be favored
due to birth right

nation state [ney-shun stayt] -noun- A state which is
sovereign and is inhabited by people who form a tight
bond and a feeling of nationality

nationalization [nash-uh-nl-i-zey-shun] -noun- The
process of bringing something, such as industry or
land, under the control of a nation

naturalization [nach-er-uh-li-zey-shun] -noun- The
process of giving someone who is an alien to a
country the rights and privilages that citizens of that
country hold

neo-classical economics   [nee-oh-klass-uh-kuhl
ek-uh-nom-iks] -noun- A theory of economics which
argues that markets should be free

Neoconservatism [nee-oh-kuhn-sur-vuh-tiz-uhm] -
noun- When people who were formally liberal or
socialist promote moderate political conservatism

———

nepotism [nep-uh-tiz-uhm] -noun- Showing favortism toward family members in business or in politics

New Deal [noo deel] -noun- Principles advocated by President Franklin D. Roosevelt for economic and social reform

New Left [noo left] -noun- A group of radical leftists in the 1960s and 1970s who wanted racial equality, nonintervention in foreign affairs, and other major economic, political, and social changes

New Right [noo rayht] -noun- A group of radical rightists who are extremely conservative in terms of defense cuts and abortion, especially

Nihilism [nahy-uh-liz-uhm] -noun- A complete rejection of any laws or institutions which are already established

non-proliferation [non-proh-lif-uh-rey-shun] -noun- The action of curbing something which is spreading widely and rapidly, such as nuclear arms

Non-Aligned Movement [non-uh-layhnd moov-ment] -noun- A group of states which do not consider themselves to be formally aligned with, or either for or against, a major power bloc

non-intervention [non-in-ter-ven-shun] -noun- A policy of a nation abstaining from interfering in the affairs of other nations or in the affairs of their own political subdivisions

nonaligned [non-uh-layhnd] -adj- Not allied with any other nation and not favoring of any other nation

nonconformist [non-kuhn-fawr-mist] -noun- A person who will not conform to the beliefs, customs, or ideas which are already established

nonpartisan [non-pahr-tuh-zuhn] -adj- Not controlled by or supporting of any certain political party or special interest group

North Atlantic Treaty Organization (NATO) -noun- In intergovernmental treaty alliance which was formed in 1949

O

oligarchy [ol-uh-gahr-kee] -noun- A government by the few, all of the power lies in a small group of individuals oligopoly [ol-i-gop-uh-lee] -noun- When there are only a few sellers in a market economy which can substantially effect other market factors

olive branch [ol-iv branch] -noun- An emblem of peace

ombudsman [ohm-buhdz-muhn] -noun- An official of the government who investigates claims made by citizens regarding other government officials or agencies

omnibus [ohm-nuh-buhs] -adj- Something which pertains to or deals with many objects at the same time

open society [oh-puhn suh-sahy-i-tee] -noun- A culture which embraces and promotes freedom of beliefs and a flexible structure

oppression [uh-presh-uhn] -noun- Authority or power that is exercised in a burdensome manner that is entirely unjust

Organization of African Unity (OAU) -noun- An organization aimed at promoting solidarity of the African nations, eradicating colonialism, raising living standards, and promoting civil rights

Organization of American States (OAS -noun- An organization aimed at promoting a feeling of unity in the United States, as well as peace and justice, collaboration, and defense of rights and independence

Organization of Economic Cooperation and Development (OECD) -noun- An organization of countries who are committed to the market economy and democracy and to coordinating domestic and international policies

Organization of Petroleum Exporting Countries (OPEC) -noun- An organization of countries who are concerned with the welfare of each as well as the best way to navigate the current oil market and keep prices stable and to negotiate fair trade

orthodoxy [awr-thuh-doks-ee] -noun- An adherence of the accepted norms, such as a religion

P

pacifism [pas-uh-fiz-uhm] -noun- An opposition to any sort of violence or war

pact [pakt] -noun- An agreement between two or more nations, groups, or people

pan African [pan af-ri-kuhn] -noun- Pertaining to Africans and African as whole concepts

pan Arab [pan ar-uhb] -noun- A political alliance or union between all Arab nations

pan Islamic [pan iz-lah-mik] -noun- A political alliance or union between all Muslim nations

panacea [pan-uh-see-uh] -noun- A cure-all for all ailments or diseases

paramilitary [par-uh-mil-uh-ter-ee] -adj- Pertaining to any group which is acting in place of a military force

parity [par-itee] -noun- Equality in status, character, or amount

parochialism [puh-roh-kee-uh-liz-uhm] -noun- The act of being excessively narrow in point of view or interests

participatory democracy [par-ti-si-puh-tor-ee dem-ok-ruh-see] -noun- Participation by citizens directly in determining decisions which will effect them economically and socially rather than allowing elected representatives to do it

partisan [pahr-tuh-zuhn] -noun- A supporter of a group or cause, especially when based on personal allegiances

partition [pahr-tish-uhn] -noun- The distribution of something into shares or portions, such as stocks

passive resistance [pass-iv re-zis-tens] -noun- Using nonviolent means to oppose the government, such as boycotts or protests

paternalism [puh-ter-nl-iz-uhm] -noun- The method of running a government which resembles the way an overly benevolent and intrusive father may deal with his children

patriarchy [pey-tree-ahr-kee] -noun- A social organization in which families, tribes, or clans are ruled by the father

patrician [puh-trish-uhn] -noun- A person of good education or of nobility, such as an aristocrat

patrimony [pa-truh-moh-nee] -noun- An estate which is inherited from one's ancestors

persona non grata [per-soh-na non grah-tah] -noun- A person who is unwelcome

petit bourgeois[pet-ee boor-zhwah-zee] -noun- In the 18th and early-19th centuries, a terms which referred to the lower middle-class

philosopher king [fi-los-uh-fer king] -noun- According to Plato, the ideal of what a king should be, enlightened and philosophically trained

pigeonhole [pij-uhn-hohl] -verb- To lay something aside for the purpose of using it at a later time

plank [plangk] -noun- The principles or objectives which are expressed on a political election platform

plebiscite [pleb-uh-sahyt -noun- A political vote which determines whether or not to get involved with another country

plenipotentiar [plen-uh-puh-ten-shee-er-ee] -noun- A diplomatic agent who has the full power or authority to conduct business matters on behalf of another person

pluralism [ploor-uh-liz-uhm] -noun- When a person holds more than one office at a time

plutocracy [ploo-tok-ruh-see] -noun- A government which is ruled by the wealthiest people

pocket veto [pok-it vee-toh] -noun- A bill which is vetoed automatically due to the president's failure to sign the bill within ten days of it being presented

polarization [poh-ler-uh-zay-shun] -noun- A division of a group into factions which are in opposition

political access [poh-lit-i-kuhl ak-sess] -noun- Having access to political figures and campaigns

political asylum [poh-lit-i-kuhl uh-si-lum] -noun- When one nation grants asylum to the refugees of another nation

political capital [poh-lit-i-kuhl kap-i-tuhl] -noun- The opinion of another person or organization about you or your organization

political realism [poh-lit-i-kuhl ree-uhl-iz-uhm] -noun- A theory which puts national security and interest over moral concerns and social reconstruction

political theory [poh-lit-i-kuhl theer-ee] -noun- An orientation which determines or characterizes the thinking of an entire group or a nation

politicization [puh-lit-uh-sahyz-ey-shun] -noun- The act of making something political populism [pop-yuh-liz-uhm] -noun- A grass-roots democracy which represents the common people in the working class

pork barrel [pohrk bar-uhl] -noun- A government's tendency to spend money on localized projects for the sole purpose of bringing in money to the representative's district

possession [puh-zesh-uhn] -noun- The actual holding or occupancy of something, whether the person holding it is the rightful owner or not

post mortem [pohst mohr-tuhm] -noun- Collected or occurring after the death of someone

pragmatic [prag-mat-ik] -adj- Pertaining to a community or state's affairs; pertaining to a point of view which is practical

preamble [pree-am-buhl] -noun- An introductory statement which precedes a deed, statute, etc.

prerogative [pre-rog-uh-tiv] -noun- The exclusive right or privilege which is given to a person of a specific category

pressure group [presh-er groop] -noun- A group of people who spreads influence by the use of propaganda and lobbying

prestige [pre-steej] -noun- A distinction or reputation which has come about due to success or achievement

price controls [prayhs kon-trohls] -noun- The government's regulation of prices by asking the maximum amount of money for products, such as in a time of inflation

prime minister [prahym min-uh-ster] -noun- The head of the government and primary minister in governments which have a parliament

prior restraint [prahy-er ri-streynt] -noun- Prevents unpublished and censored material from being published

private enterprise [prahy-vit en-ter-prahyz] -noun- A doctrine which states that a political economy can regulate itself through supply and demand with minimal intervention from the government

private sector [prahy-vit sek-tohr] -noun- The area of economy which is under the private control of individuals rather than the government privatization [prahy-vuh-tahy-zey-shun] -noun- The act of switching something from public or governmental control to a private enterprise

pro-choice [proh-chois] -noun- The support of a woman's choice when it comes to abortion, and of the legality of abortion

pro-life [proh-lahyf] -noun- A person who is opposed to the legalization of abortion

probate [proh-beyt] -noun- Proof that a will is valid and authentic, which is determined in a probate court

probation [proh-bey-shun] -noun- A period of testing of a person's conduct or qualifications

probe [prohb] -verb- To examine or explore something thoroughly

proletariat [proh-li-tair-ee-uht] -noun- The lowest and poorest class of people in a society

proportional [pruh-pawr-shuh-nl] -adj- Having the correct proportion; corresponding

prosecution [pros-i-kyoo-shuhn]   -noun- The process of carrying out legal proceedings against a person

protectionism [pruh-tek-shun-iz-uhm] -noun- A policy or program which seeks to protect the environment, wildlife, and property owners

protectorate [pruh-tek-ter-it] -noun- A strong state which protects a weaker state, and one which is may partly control

Protestant work ethic [prot-uh-stuhnt wurk eth-ik] -noun- A concept which supports the Calvinist idea that a person's hard work will lead to success as well as salvation

providence [prov-i-duhns] -noun- A manifestation of divine protection or care

provocation [prov-uh-key-shuhn] -noun- A thing which irritates, angers, incites, or instigates

proxy [prok-see] -noun- A persn with the agency or power to substitute or act as the deputy for another person

---

public morals [pub-lik mohr-uhls] -noun- The ethic and moral standards which are enforced in a society, generally by law enforcement officials or by social pressures

public opinion poll [pub-lik uh-pin-yun pohl] -noun- A poll that is taken in an effort to determine what election results are going to be, by polling a cross-section of the public

public ownership [pub-lik oh-ner-ship] -noun- Nationalization or ownership of something by the state

public sector [pub-lik sek-ter] -noun- The affairs of the nation which are under the control of the government, rather than privately controlled

public works [pub-lik wurkz] -noun- Structures which are paid for by the government and for the use of the public, such as post offices, roads, dams, etc.

puppet regime [puhp-it ruh-zheem] -noun- A government which is controlled by another government of a foreign nation

purge [perj] -verb- To legally wipe out an accusation, or offense by the use of atonement or any other action which is seen as suitable

pyrrhic victory [peer-rik vik-tor-ee] -noun- A victory which is achieved at a cost which is perhaps too high

Q

quid pro quo [kwid proh kwoh] -noun- A substitute; something that is given in place of another thing, or taken

quisling [kwiz-ling] -noun- A person who helps the enemy and in turn betrays their own country; that person will likely end up being a participate in a puppet government

quorum [kwawr-uhm] -noun- The quota of members who must be present to legally make business transactions

R

raison d'etat [re-zawn dey-ta] -noun- In French, something which is good for the entire country

raison d'etre [re-zawn de-truh] -noun- A reason for being; a justification of existence rank and file [rangk and fahyl] -noun- The members of an organization who are not leaders

ratification [rat-uh-fi-key-shuhn] -noun- The act of approving and giving sanction of an act

raw materials [raw muh-teer-ee-uhl] -noun- \A material which has not yet been processed or manufactured into your final form

reactionary [ree-ak-shuhn-er-ee] -adj- Describing a reaction which is likely in opposition to liberalism or progress

Reagan Doctrine [rey-gan dok-trin] -noun- A doctrine introduced by President Reagan which provided that the United States would offer aid to anti-Communist movements and guerillas

realism [ree-uh-liz-uhm] -noun- An inclination toward pragmatism and literal truth

Realpolitik [rey-ahl-poh-li-teek] -noun- Political realism, usually in the form of a policy which is based on power over ideals recession [ri-sesh-uhn] -noun- In economics, a period of contraction which is sometimes only limited in duration

red herring [red her-ing] -noun- Something which serves the purpose of diverted from what is the real problem

redistribution [ree-dis-truh-byoo-shuhn] -noun- In economics, a theory which promotes reducing any inequalities that may exist in the distribution of wealth

referendum [ref-uh-ren-duhm] -noun- A note that a diplomat writes to their own government asking for further instructions

refugee [ref-yoo-jee] -noun- A person who leaves their own country for the sake of safety, especially during a period of social upheaval

regime [ruh-zheem] -noun- The period of time in which a particular ruling system holds power

regionalism [ree-juh-nl-iz-uhm] -noun- The practice of dividing small areas such as cities or states into different administrative sections

___

reparations [rep-uh-rey-shuhn] -noun- Compensation payable in many different forms from one country to another after a war

repatriation [ree-pey-tree-ey-shuhn] -noun- The acting of returning a person to their own country

repression [ree-presh-uhn] -noun- Persecution of groups or individuals for political reasons

reprieve [ri-preev] -noun- A short break from any impending punishment, such as execution

reprisals [ri-prahy-zuhlz] -noun- An act of retaliation in which property or belongings can be seized from the subjects of the retaliation

republic [ree-puh-blik] -noun- Any group of people who together is considered a commonwealth

retaliation [ri-tal-ee-ey-shuhn] -noun- A pay back in kind, like for like

retroactive legislation [re-troh-ak-tiv lej-is-ley-shuhn] -noun- Laws which were designed to punish the act of tax evasion when it is seen as blatantly unethical

reverse discrimination [ri-vers dis-krim-uh-ney-shuhn] -noun- Unfair treatment which is aimed at members of majority, rather than minority, groups

revisionism [ri-vizh-uh-niz-uhm] -noun- A departure from a doctrine which is generally widely received, such as that of Marx

revolution [rev-uh-loo-shuhn] -noun- An overthrow and subsequent replacement of an established political system and government

revolutionary [rev-uh-loo-shuhn-er-ee adj-Anything which is radically new or innovative

rhetoric [ret-er-ik] -noun- The study of how to use language effectively

right wing [rahyt wing] -noun- Members of the conservative party and those who oppose political form

rubber stamp [ruhb-er stamp] -noun- An agency of the government which automatically gives approval

rule of thumb [rool uhv thuhm] -noun- A general practice which is based on experience rather than scientific calculations

ruling class [rool-ing klas] -noun- The class of people who have power over the others

S

sabotage [sab-uh-tahzh] -noun- Any underhand interference or undermining of a cause

sacred cow [sey-kred kow] -noun- Any individual or organization which is considered as exempt from any criticism

sanctions [sangk-shuhns] -noun- Authoritative approval or support for an action

sanctuary [sangk-choo-er-ee] -noun- Any place which is holy or sacred

satellite country [sat-l-ahyt kun-tree] -noun- A country which was once independent but is currently under economic and political influence of another country

scarcity [skair-si-tee] -noun- When there is a shortness in supply, or when something happens infrequently or is rare secession [si-sesh-uhn] -noun- The act of withdrawing from an alliance formally, such as political, religious, or a federation

secondary boycott [sek-uhn-der-ee boi-kot] -noun- When union members boycott their employer in an effort to get their employer to pressure another company who the union is having a problem with

secret ballot [see-krit bal-uht] -noun- A method of voting in which each person's vote is kept anonymous and secret

sectarian [sek-tair-ee-uhn] -adj- Being narrowly limited, confined, or devoted in terms of sects, interests, or purpose

secular [sek-yuh-ler] -adj- Pertaining to things which are worldly but are not associated with religion

secularization [sek-yuh-luh-rahyz-ey-shuhn]-verb-To separate something from its religious ties and to make it unspiritual or worldly

security [si-kyoor-i-tee] -noun- Precautionary measures to keep the people safe from harm, crime, attack, espionage, or sabotage

sedition [si-dish-uhn] -noun- An action, usually in writing or speech, which incites discomfort or possible rebellion with the government

self determination [self di-tur-muh-ney-shuhn] -noun- The freedom of a person to live as their choose and to make decisions and perform actions without seeking the input or permission of others, or the government, first

separation of powers [sep-uh-rey-shuhn uhv pow-ers] -noun- The idea and act of splitting the government into judicial, executive, and legislative branches

separatism [sep-er-uh-tiz-uhm] -noun- The act of being one who advocates the separation of a smaller group from the larger one, especially in political units

servitude [sur-vi-tood] -noun- Some sort of slavery or compulsory service as a form of punishment

show trials [sho tri-uhls] -noun- A trial which is shown publically generally for the use of propaganda, as a means to discourage citizens from going against the government by making an example of the person on trial

shuttle [shuht-l]-verb-To move a person or thing back and forth as though between two or more destinations

silk stocking district [sil stok-ing dis-trikt] -noun-
The Upper East Side of Manhattan; remains as one of
the most affluent areas of New York City

silver [sil-ver] -noun- A metal which is used to make
currency or is seen as a commodity

sitting on the fence [sit-ting on uh fens] -noun- A
phrase which expresses a person's ambivalence about
a subject

skinheads [skin-hedz] -noun- A group of people who
use their shaved heads as symbols of anarchy,
rebellion, and often white supremacy

social contract [so-shuhl kon-tract] -noun- An
agreement between an individual or group of people
and the government or the community as whole

social Darwinism [so-shuhl dar-win-iz-uhm] -noun-
In the 19th century, a theory which supported
Darwin's idea of survival of the fittest; the people
who survive in a society are those who are best
adapted to those particular conditions

social justice [so-shuhl jus-tis] -noun- A society in which the advantages and disadvantages are dispersed evenly

Social Security [so-shuhl suh-kyoor-uh-tee] -noun- The provision of economic security and social welfare for individuals which is achieved through government programs which are paid for by the citizen's taxes

social services [so-shuhl sur-vis-ez] -noun- The organized efforts to improve human welfare and aimed toward helping disadvantaged citizens

social stratification [so-shuhl strat-uh-fuh-key-shuhn] -noun- The hierarchy of social classes and status within a society

social welfare [so-shuhl wel-fair] -noun- The social services which a government provides for its citizens

socialism [so-shuhl-iz-uhm] -noun- A economic system in which the community has social control of the all means of production and works together to manage the economy

socialization [so-shuhl-uh-zey-shuhn] -noun- The process an individual undergoes, usually continuous, of adapting to the social norms that are appropriate for their current social position

sovereign [sov-rin] -noun- A person who has supreme power as a ruler

speculation [spek-yuh-ley-shuhn] -noun- The consideration or contemplation of a subject

sphere [sfeer] -noun- A person's walk of life, social world, or the stratum of society

stagflation [stag-fley-shuhn] -noun- A period of inflation in which unemployment is on the rise and activity of businesses becomes stagnate

standing orders   [stan-ding or-derz] -noun- The rules which state that procedure should always be followed when holding assembly

Star Wars [star-wawrz] -noun- A weapons research program in the United States in 1984 to explore technologies which could destroy missiles an warheads

stare decisis [stair-ee di-sahy-sis] -noun- A principle of law which states that judges must respect any precedents which have been established by previous decisions

START -noun- Strategic Arms Reduction Treaty; a bilateral treaty between the United States and the USSR which reduced and limited the supply and use of strategic offensive arms

states' rights [steytz rahytz] -noun- Political powers which are reserved for the state governments rather than the federal government

statesman [steytz-muhn] -noun- A person who is experienced in the government and government administration and who can direct government affairs

status quo [stat-uhs kwoh] -noun- Something which is the existing condition or state

status [stat-uhs] -noun- A person's position, often in terms of social standing, in relation to others

statute [stach-oot] -noun- A rule which is established by a corporation or organization which is put in place to govern the internal affairs

stimulus [stim-yuh-luhs] -noun- Something which incites to action or exertion, or quickens feelings or thoughts

storm in a tea cup [stohrm in uh tee-cuhp] -noun- An event which is small but has been blown out of proportion to be much bigger than it actually is

straddle the fence [strad-l tha fens] -noun- The supporting of both sides of an issue

Strategic Defense Initiative [struh-tee-jik dee-fens in-ish-yuh-tiv] -noun- A proposal by President Reagan to use systems both on the ground and in space to protect the United States from attack by nuclear ballistic missiles; Star Wars

strategy [strat-i-jee] -noun- The science of employing the means of war to plan large military movements

straw vote [straw voht] -noun- A vote which is unofficial and serves the purpose of gathering a general idea of how the public feels in regards to certain issues

strawman [straw-man -noun- A person who has no interest in a property but who receives a property anyway as a step in making the transaction more complicated in the eyes of the law

structural unemployment [struhk-chur-uhl un-em-ploi-ment] -noun- Unemployment which comes from economic changes, such as demographics or technology

subpoena [suh-pee-nuh] -noun- A writ which summons a person, evidence, or documents to court for the purpose of witness

subsidy   [suhb-si-dee] -noun- A fund which is aided to a private industry, a charity, or the like by the government

subsistence [suhb-sis-tens] -noun- A means of supporting live or livelihood

subversive [suhb-vur-siv] -adj- Intended to overthrow an already established government

succession [suhk-sesh-uhn] -noun- The process by which one person takes over another person's role, rank, position, etc.

suffrage [suhf-rij] -noun- A person's right to vote, especially in elections which are political

summit [suhm-it] -noun- In government, the highest level of official or diplomat

superpower [soo-per-pou-er] -noun- A nation which has extreme power to influence international events and the policies of nations which are much smaller

supply and demand [suh-pley and duh-mand] -noun- The relationship between how much of a product is available and the demand for the product which determines what the price will be

surplus value [sur-pluhs val-yoo] -noun- The value of a product which exceeds the cost of making it, which is considered a profit to the capitalist

symposium [sim-poh-zee-uhm] -noun- A meeting attended by several minds where a topic is discussed thoroughly by each member

syndicalism [sin-di-kuhl-iz-uhm] -noun- In economics, a system in which the workers own and manage their industry

T

taboo [ta-boo] -adj- Prohibited from practice or from use, or seen by society as unacceptable

tariff [tar-if] -noun- The taxes which are imposed on imports and exports by the government

Tea Party [tee par-tee] -noun- A political movement in the United States imposed by the conservatives stating opposition to taxes and government spending

territorial waters [tar-uh-toh-ree-uhl wah-ters] -noun- The waters, generally within three miles of land, which are under the jurisdiction of the littoral states

terrorism [ter-uh-riz-uhm] -noun- To intimidate or coerce the government by means of threats and violence, especially in politics

theocracy [thee-ok-ruh-see] -noun- A form of government in which God, a deity, or some sort of higher spiritual power, is seen as ruler

third party [thurd par-tee -noun- A political party which is formed with members who do not identify specifically with either of the two dominating parties

total war [toh-tahl wawr] -noun- A war in which all available supplies, resources, and weaponry are employed

totalitarianism [toh-tal-i-tair-ee-uhn-iz-uhm] -noun- A state or governing branch of a centralized institution which holds complete control and absolute power

tribunal [trahy-byoo-nuhl] -noun- A place of judgment such as a court of law

truce [troos] -noun- An agreement which establishes a suspension of war or hostilities for a specified amount of time

Truman Doctrine [troo-muhn dok-trin] -noun- The policy of President Truman to give aid to countries affected by Communist, such as Greece and Turkey

trusteeship [truh-stee-ship] -noun- When the United Nations grants a country administrative control of a territory

tyranny   [tir-uh-nee] -noun- A government which is ruled severely and unjustly by an absolute ruler

U

underground [uhn-der-ground] -noun- A organization which is held in secret to fight an already established government

unilateral [yoo-nuh-lat-er-uhl] -adj- An undertaking or decision made by only one side of a party or faction

united front [yoo-nahy-tid fruhnt] -noun- A coalition which serves the purpose of united against a menacing force that effects community interest

universalism [yoo-nuh-vur-suh-liz-uhm] -noun- Having a character, knowledge or interest which applies to all people

usurpation [yoo-ser-pey-shuhn] -noun- The illegal seizure and subsequent occupation of a power position

usury [yoo-zhuh-ree] -noun- Lending money with a huge rate of interest attached

utilitarianism [yoo-til-uh-tair-ee-uhn-iz-uhm] -noun- A doctrine stating that every action and means of conduct should be aimed toward the greater good and a promotion of universal happiness

utility [yoo-til-i-tee] -noun- The quality or state of being useful, such as a public service

V

vanguard [van-gahrd] -noun- The leaders of any movement, especially political or intellectual

Vatican Councils [vat-uh-kin cown-sil] -noun- Councils which dealt with the rising issues of liberalism, rationalism, and materialism

vendetta [ven-det-uh] -noun- A prolonged feud or rivalry, often in connection to a murder or betrayal

veto [vee-toh]-verb-The act of rejected or prohibiting something, such as a congressional bill

vicious circle [vish-uhs sur-kuhl] -noun- A situation in which trying to better a problem only aggravates it further or creates a new, more severe problem

vigilante [vij-uh-lan-tee] -noun- A person who takes vengeance and the law into their own hands and their own control

visa [vee-suh] -noun- An endorsement made by an official representative which allows a person entrance into another country upon the acceptance of a passport

W

war crime [wawr krahym] -noun- Crimes which are committed against prisoners of war or enemies which go against the international agreements or are offensive to humanity as a whole

ward heeler [wahrd hee-ler] -noun- A member of a political party who does chores, such as canvassing voters, for the bigger political bosses

Warsaw Pact [wawr-saw pakt] -noun- Organization between the USSR, Poland, Bulgaria, East Germany, Hungary, Czechoslovakia, and Romania which united the countries under a collective defense a joint command of military forces

ways and means [weyz and meenz] -noun- Methods and legislation created to raise revenue for government use

welfare[wel-fair] -noun- The health, happiness, and prosperity of an individual or group, or financial assistance given to a family

welfare state [wel-fair stayt] -noun- A state which is responsible for the welfare of the general public in terms of finances, education, health, housing, and working conditions

westernization [wes-ter-nahy-zey-shuhn] -noun- The process of adapting customs and practices to mirror those of the United States

whip [wip] -noun- In a legislative body, a party manager who is responsible for securing voting attendance

white elephant [wahyt el-uh-fuhnt] -noun- Something which costs the owner a fair amount of money, disproportionate to its use

world government [wurld guhv-ern-muhnt] -noun- The idea of having one single political and governing party which will serve all of the world

World Bank [wurld bangk] -noun- A specialized agency of the United States; a international bank which gives loans to help member nations to reconstruct and to develop

X

xenophobia [zen-uh-foh-bee-uh] -noun- An unreasonable and unfounded fear of foreigners

Y

yardstick [yahrd-stik] -noun- A standard of judgment
and measurement

Z

zealot [zehl-uht] -noun- A fanatic; a member of a
radical Jewish group which wanted to violently
overthrow Roman rule in 69-81 a.d.

Zeitgeist [tsahyt-gahyst] -noun- In German, a nation's
general feeling that is characteristic of a certain point
in time

zero sum [zeer-oh-suhm] -noun- An economy in
which the sum of the financial gains is equal to the
sum of the losses

Zionism [zahy-uh-niz-uhm] -noun- A Jewish
movement which spread worldwide and led to the
establishment of the state of Israel

www.ingramcontent.com/pod-product-compliance
Lightning Source LLC
Chambersburg PA
CBHW071327310526
45789CB00016B/1227